THE STORY OF BRITAIN: IN TUDOR AND STUART TIMES

The author's lively approach to history and the artist's brilliant illustrations in both colour and black and white brings the past vividly to life in *The Story of Britain*, which was originally published as one volume.

The author, R. J. Unstead, is renowned as 'the young reader's historian'. He wrote his first book, *Looking at History*, when he was the headmaster of a school in Hertfordshire.

The artist, Victor Ambrus, has illustrated many books for children and has been awarded the Kate Greenaway Medal of the Library Association.

3 cde

THE STORY OF BRITAIN:
IN TUDOR AND STUART TIMES

R. J. UNSTEAD

THE STORY OF BRITAIN: IN TUDOR AND STUART TIMES

Illustrated by Victor Ambrus
Carousel Editor: Anne Wood

TRANSWORLD PUBLISHERS LTD
A National General Company

THE STORY OF BRITAIN: IN TUDOR AND STUART TIMES

A CAROUSEL BOOK 0 552 54003 X

Originally published in Great Britain
by Adam and Charles Black Ltd.

PRINTING HISTORY
Adam and Charles Black edition (one volume entitled
The Story of Britain, which forms the Carousel edition
of *The Story of Britain: In Tudor and Stuart Times*
and the companion Carousel volumes *The Story of Britain:
Before the Norman Conquest, In the Middle Ages*, and *From
William of Orange to World War II*) published 1969

Carousel edition published 1971
Carousel edition reprinted 1971

Carousel Books are published by Transworld
Publishers Ltd.
Cavendish House, 57–59 Uxbridge Road,
Ealing, London, W.5

Made and printed in Great Britain by
Cox & Wyman Ltd., London, Reading and Fakenham

CONTENTS

THE FIRST OF THE TUDORS

WHEN, on Bosworth Field, the 'crown of ornament' was placed on Henry Tudor's head, the new King had seen almost nothing of the kingdom he was to rule for the rest of his life. Half of his twenty-eight years had been spent in Wales and the rest in exile. Yet this wary, clever stranger, more Welsh than English, was exactly the man whom England needed.

To begin with Henry VII was not a warrior. He would fight if he had to but, for exercise, he preferred hunting and he liked books, music and the business of the kingdom, especially its money-accounts, better than tournaments and costly ceremonies. The country wanted peace, and he sensed that if he restored the force of law and settled the Yorkist-Lancastrian feud, he

might keep the crown he had won by daring and treachery.

So he fulfilled his oath to marry Elizabeth of York, the tall, blue-eyed sister of the two Princes who had disappeared in Richard III's reign. The marriage did not put an end to all the Yorkist plots, but from now on they flourished only in those parts which lived on discord and pillage – the northern and the Welsh borders.

As long as the great lords kept private armies to terrorize their neighbours and to overcome the law-courts, there could be no settled peace. But, crippled by their losses in the recent wars, the barons were obliged to obey Henry when he ordered them to dismiss their armed retainers. A few had forgotten the need for obedience to a royal command and, early in the reign when Henry paid a visit to the Earl of Oxford, he found himself greeted by a guard of honour wearing the Oxford badge.

'These are your servants?' inquired the King.

'They are my retainers, assembled here to do you honour,' replied Oxford proudly.

'I thank you for your hospitality,' said Henry, 'but I like not to have my laws broken in my own sight.'

Shortly afterwards, Oxford was summoned to appear before a special court which fined him £15,000, a sum so immense that it convinced the barons that it was wiser to obey the law than to risk the King's displeasure.

But it took more than fines and a successful marriage to make the throne secure. For fifteen years Henry had to overcome his difficulties by skill and cunning, for there were enemies in Ireland, France and Flanders, besides rivals in the Tower and friends at home who would change sides the moment he lost his grip.

A baker's son named Lambert Simnel who claimed to be Edward Plantagenet, was crowned in Ireland but

Henry routed the boy's supporters and contemptuously put young Simnel to work in the royal kitchen. Presently, the Yorkists tried again. This time they produced Perkin Warbeck, a handsome youth who gave out that he was Richard of York and had escaped from the Tower when his elder brother was murdered. From Ireland, Warbeck made his way to Flanders where Margaret of York 'recognized' him as her nephew. Henry countered by threatening to stop the Flemish wool trade, so Warbeck took himself to Scotland where he found favour and a bride of noble birth.

By this time, Henry had discovered that Sir William Stanley, whose treachery had given him the victory at Bosworth, was again playing a double game. Without a moment's hesitation, he had his old friend arrested and executed. Meanwhile, a rising of discontented Cornishmen persuaded Warbeck to try his luck in the West Country but when Henry came down with an army, the rebellion fizzled out. A few of the leaders were hanged but the rest were heavily fined and Warbeck himself was treated with mercy until his own folly brought him to the Tower and death by hanging.

After this Henry's difficulties became less. Almost every rival had been killed off and he was able to concentrate upon making the throne safe for his son. Money was the key to power and he set himself to gather in wealth by every possible means. A foreigner described him as 'a great miser but a man of vast ability'. He punished offenders with fines and, as his love of gold increased, he also suggested that his subjects should make 'gifts' to their royal master. To his collectors he pointed out that a man who lived in style could obviously afford to make a rich gift and a man who lived plainly must have money saved away. In either case, he had to pay! When Henry invaded France with a powerful army, he accepted a vast sum from the French King and went home without fighting, much to the disgust of his own nobles who had half-ruined themselves to provide men and equipment for the campaign.

Under this wily King, the country prospered and foreign monarchs had a new respect for England's friendship. So Henry was able to marry his eldest son Arthur to Catherine of Aragon, daughter of the King of Spain, and his daughter Margaret to the Scottish King, James IV. But Henry's interest in affairs outside England was not shared by his own countrymen.

Christopher Columbus's immortal voyage of 1492 and the Portuguese discovery of a sea-route to India aroused no excitement in the English captains. Their greatest exploits were to sail their ships to fish off the

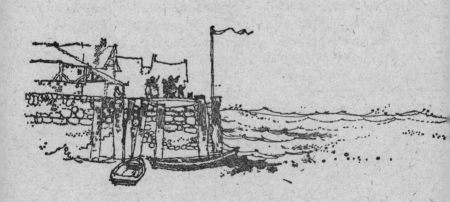

Iceland coast or to trade across the narrow seas with Gascony, Flanders and the Baltic ports.

There was living in Bristol, however, a citizen of Venice, Giovanni Caboto, otherwise John Cabot who, like Columbus, had been born in Genoa and had the same notion that the spicelands of the East could be reached by sailing west across the Atlantic. His ideas aroused some interest but no financial support until Henry VII paid a visit to Bristol. Cabot was invited to explain his plans for a voyage of discovery to the King, who was already aware that his fellow monarchs of Portugal and Spain were on the threshold of riches that would make his own hoard seem like a handful of pennies. Henry offered to provide a ship in which Cabot could put his theories to the test.

In 1497 the *Mathew*, a tiny vessel with a crew of
eighteen, sailed out of Bristol and headed westward into
the Atlantic Ocean. Several weeks later the lookout
sighted a 'new-found land', a bleak grey headland which
Cabot imagined to be the northern tip of Asia. It was
in fact the coast of North America, the continent whose
existence neither Cabot nor Columbus ever suspected or
indeed recognized. Ashore, there was no sign of life apart
from a few bone needles and primitive traps. The sea
was teeming with great codfish which could be pulled
inboard by the basket-load but since he had not come
for fish, Cabot sailed for home to report his meagre discovery and to ask for a larger ship so that he could go on
next time to Cathay itself.

King Henry rewarded the Genoese captain with a
pension and in the following year Cabot set out again
with a small fleet of ships provided by the King and
several enterprising merchants. Once again he reached
the American mainland and this time he coasted south-
ward, looking hopefully for a channel that would lead
him to the land of silks and spices. He never found it and
must have returned to Bristol a puzzled and disappointed man, for no more is heard of him except that he
drew his pension a year later. The merchants left no
mention of him either; perhaps they decided to cut their
losses and to say nothing for fear of discouraging
others.

The King did not lose all interest in ocean voyages.
Never a man to waste money, he awarded £10 a year to
John's son, Sebastian Cabot, 'for diligent services in and
about the port of Bristol'. Sebastian, a smooth-tongued
fellow with a flair for extracting money from royal
pockets, afterwards claimed that he had explored the
coast of North America but it seems likely that he was 'a
teller of other men's tales', and in the next reign he took

himself off to Spain where he prospered greatly and became Pilot-Major to the King of Spain.

Henry VII died in 1509, a sad figure whose last years were darkened by illness and the deaths of his wife and eldest son. His popularity had gone and his ministers were hated for their greed. But he left a vigorous, well-run kingdom and in the Treasury there was said to be a million pounds.

HENRY VIII

THE new monarch, Henry VIII, was not quite eighteen. In the eyes of his delighted subjects here was the very picture of all that a king should be. A magnificent athlete, six feet two inches tall, Henry was the most handsome and talented Prince in Europe. He spoke French, Latin, Italian and Spanish; he liked mathematics, he wrote poetry, played several instruments and composed music. At tennis, archery, jousting and riding, there was scarcely anyone to equal him, and at dancing he leapt and pirouetted faster and higher than all the courtiers. His father had kept him hard at his books, but now this great handsome boy, blessed with all the skills and learning of the age, burst upon the scene eager to make up for lost time by enjoying himself and impressing the world with his grandeur.

The old King's money was not allowed to lie in the

treasury. Young Henry spent it with fabulous extravagance in a riot of tournaments, feasting, dancing and entertainments which followed his accession to the throne. In more serious vein, he did two things to please the people. He gave orders that his father's most unpopular ministers should have their heads cut off and he married Catherine of Aragon, the widow of his brother Arthur.

The Pope gave permission for the marriage and Catherine, a grey-eyed beauty whose gaiety and love of dancing won the hearts of the English, delighted her eager husband. For the moment all was happiness in England and at court. It was not long before Henry decided to win glory in a war against France and when the older members of his council advised against the adventure, he speedily found an ambitious newcomer who was only too ready to carry out his wishes.

Thomas Wolsey came from Ipswich where his father, a grazier and butcher, was in a good way of business, for young Thomas had been sent to college at Oxford and into the Church. He was clever and he rose fast in the world. From tutor to a nobleman's sons, he became chaplain and secretary to the Archbishop of Canterbury and then to the old King himself.

Thus, when Henry VIII looked round at his council, he noted among the greybeards this young priest of brilliant talents and unquenchable greed. The minister to whom he gave his friendship was speedily raised above all the others and while Henry enjoyed himself, Wolsey managed the kingdom. With enormous gusto, he took on the arrangements for the French war and raised an army to enable Henry to cut a glorious figure on the Continent. The start was disappointing but in due course he managed to provide Henry with the desired victory, even if it was not a second Agincourt. The

French rode away so fast that the fight was called the Battle of the Spurs! However, a few towns were captured and Henry had the satisfaction of knowing that Europe had seen an English king in action once again.

Meanwhile, a much greater victory was won at home when James IV of Scotland, taking advantage of his brother-in-law's absence, invaded England with a large army. As Regent, Queen Catherine met the threat with great spirit. She dispatched the old Earl of Surrey to the border with orders to raise the men of the northern counties, and at the Battle of Flodden the English longbow won its last great victory and artillery had one of its first triumphs. The Scots were utterly routed and James IV perished on the field with a dozen earls and most of his nobles. Scotland came to be governed by the widowed Queen, Margaret, whose son James V was not born until after his father's death.

The war with France was never more than a halfhearted affair, for Henry quickly realized that his crafty allies expected him to do the fighting while they reaped the gains. So he and Wolsey turned the tables by making peace and sending Henry's beautiful sister Mary to marry the old French King. He soon died, however, and was succeeded by Francis I, a King as young and masterful as Henry himself. Indeed, if Francis was less handsome, he was even richer and more warlike.

Wolsey arranged a meeting between the two rivals who, pretending nothing but gallant friendship for each other, put on a three weeks' display of such gorgeous extravagance that it was called the Field of the Cloth of Gold. Wolsey's own splendour astonished the French and added to his sovereign's glory, but all was for show and none of the chivalrous play was sincere. Henry was already plotting with the Emperor Charles, and when it

came to war, the English fought the French as they had always done.

In all these affairs, Wolsey was the master-figure who zealously managed the King's business and grew ever richer on the rewards that fell into his lap. Most of the gifts were high positions in the Church which cost Henry nothing – bishoprics, deaneries and dozens of rectorships with acres of land and fat incomes. At the height of his power, Wolsey was Bishop of Tournai, Bishop of Lincoln, Archbishop of York and Lord Chancellor of England. The Pope made him a Cardinal; he dined in state like the King and lived in a style more splendid than the greatest noblemen of Europe. He governed the kingdom, ruled the Church, built palaces, houses, a college at Oxford and a school at Ipswich. His power was immense because it was the King's power and as long as it pleased the King to have so fine a chancellor, Wolsey was the greatest man in the land. The people could curse him for the taxes and the lords could hate him for his arrogance, but while he stood in the royal favour, none could harm him. It was already clear that their handsome Prince had grown into a masterful King as cold and ruthless as any who had ever worn the crown.

MASTER OF HIS KINGDOM

BY his mid-thirties Henry was an anxious man. He and Catherine, married now for eighteen years, had but one child, a clever, delicate girl named Mary. Five other children had died in babyhood and Henry longed for a son to whom he could hand on the kingdom and the Tudor name. Other men had sons but why not he? Had he sinned in marrying his brother's widow and was this his punishment? The doubt which had entered his mind grew mightily when he fell in love with Anne Boleyn, a lady of the court. She was young and pretty, with dark eyes and black shining hair, and Henry was certain that she would give him the son he wanted. He would divorce Catherine and marry Anne. Wolsey must make the necessary arrangements with the Pope.

For kings and princes, these matters could often be settled without trouble, but just at this time the Pope was in a most difficult position. The city of Rome was occupied by the Emperor's troops and the Emperor Charles V was none other than Catherine's nephew. So, whereas the Pope wished to oblige Henry, he dared not offend Charles. The matter was delayed for weeks and

months and, try as he might, Wolsey was unable to
obtain the answer which his master desired.

At length, a cardinal came from Rome to hear the
case but delay followed delay until the King could no
longer contain his fury. All his life he had had his way
but now it seemed as if his dearest wish was to be denied.
The fault must be Wolsey's. He struck him down sav-
agely, banishing him from the court and stripping him
of most of his wealth and appointments.

Wolsey retired to York but the King's wrath followed
him and, charged with treason, he was on his way back
to London when he died at Leicester, murmuring the

regrets which he never felt in his days of power: 'Had I but served God as diligently as I have served the King, he would not have given me over in my grey hairs.'

Having broken Wolsey, Henry gave the chancellorship to Sir Thomas More and called a parliament which he knew would support his defiance of the Pope. He then put Queen Catherine aside and had Archbishop Cranmer announce his marriage to Anne Boleyn. She was crowned at Westminster with the utmost magnificence. But the people gave 'ill looks' to her as she passed by in procession.

Parliament declared the marriage legal and Henry

was made 'Supreme Head on earth, under God, of the Church of England'. The leading men of the kingdom were required to swear an oath accepting these changes and almost all of them did so. But among the few who refused the oath was Sir Thomas More, the kindly scholar who had already resigned from his position as chancellor. No parliament, he said, could appoint the head of the Church. The Duke of Norfolk told him that if he persisted in such talk, his life was as good as lost. 'Is that all, my lord?' replied More. 'Then I die today and you tomorrow.' On the scaffold, he called out calmly to the spectators, 'I die, the King's faithful servant, but God's first.'

After More's execution, the King's mastery was unopposed. He found, in Thomas Cromwell, a minister as grasping and diligent as Wolsey and, between them, they closed the monasteries, seized their wealth and sold their lands to the highest bidders. Thus, although the King kept to most of the forms of the old religion and had no liking for the new faith of those who called themselves Protestants, there were now many persons in England who did not want to see the Pope's authority restored. If that happened, they would have to give back the Church lands they had bought.

But, in the north, where the monasteries had not been hated or despised, a rebellion broke out, known as the Pilgrimage of Grace because the rebels were accompanied by priests carrying crucifixes and sacred banners. Henry dealt with the rising in his own fashion. Having dispersed the peasants and weavers with fair promises, he pounced on their leaders and had them executed without mercy.

Henceforward, no one was safe. The jovial monarch had become a suspicious despot who made and broke men as he pleased, a tyrant with more real power than any ruler of England before or since. In his portraits he stands like an arrogant bull, his vast frame made even broader by bolstered sleeves, his small eyes and pursed mouth conveying the cruelty of his character.

He was as ruthless in his private life as in public. On the night when he heard of poor Catherine's death, he laughed aloud and danced merrily with Anne Boleyn. But Anne failed him. She gave him a daughter, Elizabeth, but both her sons were born dead, so she was executed on a trumped-up charge of faithlessness. Soon he married Jane Seymour who died giving birth to Edward, his longed-for son, and some time later he permitted Thomas Cromwell to arrange an alliance with the German states and a royal marriage to a German princess. When the lady proved to be ugly, she was put aside and Cromwell was beheaded for *his* failure. Execution also ended the life of his fifth wife, the lovely, sinful Catherine Howard.

On every side, Henry was hated and feared. Yet Englishmen still regarded him with a kind of terrified admiration; they liked their King to have power and Henry's power was immense. He defied the Pope and two great monarchs abroad; Wales was subdued, Ireland brought to temporary obedience and Scotland humbled by another disastrous defeat at Solway Moss. The shame affected the Scottish King so deeply that he died, leaving a baby daughter who was later to be called Mary Queen of Scots.

Near the end of his reign, Henry heaved his great bulk into a new suit of armour and took an army to France where he captured Boulogne and came home well pleased with himself.

The French King, bent upon revenge, assembled a great fleet to invade England and it was as well that Henry had long been a builder of ships and dockyards and had spent some of the monasteries' wealth on building castles to defend the coast. Portsmouth was threatened, some small towns were burnt and a few Frenchmen got ashore, but the English ships, watched by the King himself, headed off the enemy fleet and caused it to retire. The English were disappointed. From as far afield as Worcester and Norwich, they had come marching towards the coast. King Harry might be an old tyrant but, with all his faults, he had their loyalty and they would have fought for him. Bald, immensely stout and plagued by an ulcer in his leg that was killing him, he still inspected his ships, troops and forts and was hoisted into the saddle to go 'hawking for pheasants'. His temper was vile but his brain was as keen as ever and he realized all too well the kingdom's real weakness.

The power was his and his alone. If he should die, whom could he trust to rule the land until Edward came of age? The boy was not yet ten, so Henry chose a council of ministers to carry out his desires. He picked them carefully. Men of the old religion were included and some of the new Protestant faith. There were to be no more violent changes and, during the days before his death, Henry earnestly explained to the council how they should govern the kingdom.

Then, clutching Cranmer's hand to express repentance for his sins, he died. His reign had lasted for thirty-eight years.

EDWARD VI AND LADY JANE GREY

NO sooner had Edward VI, the boy-king, been brought to London than the council began to disobey their dead master. Within a fortnight, a party of extreme Protestants had taken charge; and their leader, Jane Seymour's brother, made himself Protector and Duke of Somerset. They attacked the Roman Catholic religion and seized the remainder of Church property with a greed that would have shocked Thomas Cromwell himself. Riots and risings broke out and there was more disorder in one year than in the whole of King Henry's reign. Somerset was overthrown and executed by John Dudley, presently Duke of Northumberland, who became master of the kingdom and of young Edward.

The country fell into chaos. With their religion attacked and the King's authority gone, the people were distracted. Hooligans broke into the churches to smash ornaments and priceless stained-glass windows; the ruling class plundered the possessions of the ancient gilds and schools; rents and prices rose and the value of wages fell. England was well-nigh bankrupt.

In this situation, Northumberland's policy was merely to increase his own power. This dark ruthless man dominated everyone and, by playing upon the young King's enthusiasm for the Protestant religion and allowing no one else to come near to him, he gained a powerful hold upon the boy's mind. Until he was fifteen, Edward seemed to be quite healthy but after an attack of measles, he began to show unmistakable signs of lung disease. His illness, aggravated by the poisonous medicines of the time, rapidly became worse and he clearly had not long to live. The heir to the throne was Princess Mary, Henry's elder daughter and, after her, the Princess Elizabeth. Next in line was Henry's niece, Frances, Duchess of Suffolk, whose daughter was Lady Jane Grey.

Northumberland easily persuaded the Duchess to pass her claim to her daughter and he next arranged for Jane to marry his own son, Guilford Dudley. Jane, a clever gentle girl, was only sixteen and she had no liking for Northumberland's spoilt son, but her scheming parents, the Suffolks, set upon her so cruelly that she was forced to accept him.

All that Northumberland had to do now was to get Mary and Elizabeth out of the way. By wheedling and threatening, he persuaded the dying King to make a will leaving the kingdom to Lady Jane Grey. The Privy Council was bullied into accepting this illegal scheme, and as soon as Edward died Northumberland proclaimed his own daughter-in-law Queen of England. When she heard his words, Lady Jane cried out in anguish:

'No! No! The crown is not my right. The Lady Mary is the rightful Queen!'

Her objections were ignored and with Guilford Dudley at her side, she was taken in state to the capital.

She was so tiny that she was made to wear three-inch soles on her shoes to appear taller, but the people glowered silently at the luckless girl whom Northumberland had foisted upon them.

During her nine days' reign, Jane showed unexpected strength of character and it was her refusal to allow her father to leave London that hastened Northumberland's downfall and her own. On proclaiming Jane, he had tried to seize Princess Mary but she had ridden to Framlingham Castle in Suffolk and the men of East Anglia were soon up in arms for old Harry's daughter. Since Jane would not send her father to fight, Northumberland himself marched north with an army. By the time he reached Cambridge, his men were deserting and the game was up. Taken to the Tower, he was executed without delay and he met his end most shamefully, even denying the Protestant faith for which he had committed his crimes. Jane watched him scornfully from her prison window:

T–B

'I pray God,' she said, 'I nor no friend of mine die so miserably.' A few months later she accepted death with far more courage. Mary's advisers warned that as long as Jane was alive there would be plots and rebellion, but the Queen had no wish to execute her cousin and hoped she might become a Catholic. Jane refused and, at the age of sixteen, she was beheaded for treason on Tower Hill Green.

MARY

MARY was nearing middle-age when she came to the throne. Years of sorrow and humiliation had given her a rather severe expression but she was brave and by nature kinder than the rest of the Tudors. The people had liked her mother, Catherine of Aragon, and they admired the courageous way in which Mary had faced Northumberland. If she had acted discreetly and had brought in changes one by one, all might have been well, for many people disliked the New Prayer Book and the Protestants.

However, Mary had set her heart upon bringing England back to the Pope's authority with all speed, and the

very dangers which faced her only increased her determination to carry out what she believed to be right. At
first Parliament supported her. The Commons agreed
that Church services should be as they were in Henry
VIII's last years; Catholic bishops were released from
prison and the leading Protestants were removed from
office. But no effort was made to return the Church
lands.

The Queen's fatal mistake was to marry her cousin,
Philip of Spain. She could not or would not understand
the English dislike of seeing their country become a
small part of the great Spanish empire. The marriage
was unpopular and the Spanish priests and servants who
accompanied Philip to England were hooted at and as-
saulted in the streets. The arrival of Cardinal Pole from
Rome only made things worse, but Mary and her advisers were not dismayed by opposition. For the good of
their souls, the English would have to be taught obedience.

Persecution of the Protestants began with the burning
of Bishop Hooper and John Rogers at Smithfield and by
the end of the year some seventy persons had died. They
included Bishops Latimer and Ridley, who perished at
the same stake from which Latimer cried out:

'Be of good cheer and play the man, brother Ridley.
We shall this day light such a candle, by God's grace, in
England as I trust shall never be put out!'

Cranmer, now old and never very firm of purpose,
almost gave Mary and Pole their greatest triumph, for
he confessed his errors and agreed that he was the cause
of all the ills the Church had suffered. However, at the
end, he regained his courage and went to the stake a
Protestant, thrusting first into the flames 'that unworthy
hand' which had signed the confession.

Altogether about 300 persons were burnt alive, not

many by continental standards, but nearly all were humble folk and their persecution aroused much wider indignation than if the victims had belonged to the upper class. Mary's own life was a tragedy. Her husband left her in order to attend to affairs in Spain, the child she longed for was never born, her religion came to be hated with terrible intensity and, persuaded by Philip to declare war on France, she had to bear the blame for losing Calais, the last English possession abroad. Seriously ill and crushed by her unhappiness, she died in 1558 after a reign of only five years.

ELIZABETH

HENRY VIII's second daughter, Elizabeth, had been closely guarded throughout both the previous reigns and on more than one occasion it was only her courage and sharp wits that had saved her from the scaffold.

She was now twenty-five, red-haired and handsome rather than pretty, with a curved nose, arching brows and piercing green eyes. Though her father had neglected her, he had seen that she was well educated, and she possessed his love of sport and music. From him, too, she inherited the power to dazzle all comers, to dominate the court and to bear herself like a monarch. Yet she could fling back a jest to a tipsy carter in the crowd and outswear the Thames watermen. She had Henry's zest for life, his awful temper and some of his meanness but none of his heartless cruelty. During the next forty-five years, never fully trusting anyone, never revealing the secrets of her mind, she was to inspire love and obedience such as the nation had rarely given to a man and never before to a woman.

At the time of her accession, her chances of survival seemed small. The people were not yet devoted to her and there was bitter enmity between Catholics and Protestants. If she seemed to favour one side more than the other, she was likely to invite a rebellion or a foreign invasion and she had not the soldiers or the ships to deal with either.

King Philip of Spain was naturally interested in adding his dead wife's kingdom to his empire and he offered to marry Elizabeth. She had no intention of ac-

cepting him, but was careful not to offend him by a blank refusal.

At this time, however, France was more dangerous than Spain. The French King, Henry II, had recently captured Calais and was thirsting for further success. He already had a powerful hold on Scotland where Mary Queen of Scots' mother, a French princess, was ruling the country with the aid of French troops. Henry II had married his son to Mary Queen of Scots who, in Catholic eyes, was the rightful Queen of England. It would suit the French King very well to unite both kingdoms and to keep them under his own control.

In this dangerous situation, Elizabeth played her cards cleverly. At home, she managed to settle the religious question in a way that did not please either the Protestants or the Catholics very much but did not drive them to rebellion. She said that people could pray as they pleased, so long as they did not upset the state, and she would have no more persecution. In the first eleven years of her reign, not one person was burnt for religion or executed for treason. As for Philip, she knew that he would not let his great enemy, the French King, put Mary Queen of Scots on the English throne, so she kept on friendly terms with him and let him go on hoping that she would marry him one day.

In Scotland she was lucky. John Knox, a fiery Protestant, returned from exile and within a year his preaching had filled the Lowland Scots with such hatred of the Roman Catholic religion that, with sly help from Elizabeth, they drove out the French soldiers and freed Scotland from French influence.

Henry II's fleet carrying fresh troops to Edinburgh was destroyed by a gale and he himself died from an injury received in a tournament. His son became King Francis II, and Mary Queen of Scots was now Queen of France and, she claimed, Queen of England too. For the moment, Elizabeth's danger was worse than ever.

However, the young King died suddenly and Mary found herself no longer welcome at the French court. She therefore returned to Scotland, a country she had not seen since babyhood.

Mary was nineteen, a gay and beautiful girl whose misfortune was to have no wise counsellors to guide her. At first she tried hard to win the hearts of the people and to come to friendly terms with Knox, but it was not long before she made the disastrous mistake of marrying her cousin, Lord Darnley. This not only aroused the envy of other Scottish nobles but Darnley soon proved himself to be an arrogant waster. His own wife despised him and gave him no part in ruling the kingdom so, in a jealous rage, he burst into the Queen's room with a gang of ruffians, who dragged out her Italian secretary, David Rizzio, and murdered him. Not long afterwards Darnley himself was found dead in the garden of a house just outside Edinburgh. Whether Mary had any part in the plot is not known; at all events, the Earl of Bothwell, a handsome dare-devil, was charged with the crime and acquitted, thanks to the presence of his own troopers in the capital.

Three months later, Mary married Bothwell. Blinded by love, she seemed to have no idea that people regarded him as a murderer or that her own conduct had filled them with angry disgust. The Scots drove her from the throne in favour of her infant son James and imprisoned her in a castle on an island in Loch Leven.

One evening, her page-boy, Willie Douglas, stole the governor's keys, unlocked Mary's room and led her to the water's edge where they scrambled into a small boat and rowed across the loch to a group of waiting friends. In Glasgow, Mary raised an army but her troops were defeated by the Scottish Regent and she galloped away to avoid capture. Unable to find a ship to take her to France, she made for England to demand help from Elizabeth.

The English Queen, embarrassed by the fugitive's arrival, followed her usual custom of not giving a definite answer to a difficult problem. If she helped Mary to regain her throne, the Protestants would be up in arms. If she handed her back to her captors, Catholics everywhere would be furious and, if she let her go abroad,

Mary would certainly try to obtain armed help from
Spain and France. To avoid trouble, it was best to do
nothing at all. So Elizabeth refused to see her cousin and
kept her, half-guest, half-prisoner, in various northern
castles for the next nineteen years.

Mary, whose beauty and health faded as the years of
captivity went by, never lost her courage or the devotion
of her friends to whom she wrote incessant letters ap-
pealing for help. Plans of escape and plots to recover her
throne filled her days and nights, but there were spies
watching her and informers paid to pass every scrap of
information, including the letters which she believed to
be secret, to Elizabeth's agents.

Meanwhile, at the English court, Elizabeth held the
stage like a great actress. Surrounded by a brilliant
company of nobles, ambassadors, poets, musicians and
adventurers, she played whatever part suited her mood –
imperious monarch, scholarly Queen, huntress, love-sick
maiden or boisterous hoyden. She adored the flattery of
handsome young men, but never lost her head like Mary
and never trusted the real business of the kingdom to
these splendid gallants, not even to her favourite, the
Earl of Leicester. Serious matters were discussed with
Mr Secretary Cecil, her faithful, tireless minister,
though her tantrums and refusal to make up her mind
often filled him and the Council with despair. In fact,
she understood far better than her ministers the value of
deceit and delay. She fended off her enemies by guile
because England was not yet strong enough to defy them
in war.

There was one matter in which the Queen exasperated everyone. Her ministers and Parliament wanted
her to marry and provide England with a son and heir of
the Protestant faith. This, they thought, would put an
end to Catholic plots. But although the suitors came and

went – princes and dukes from France, Spain, Sweden, Germany, Scotland and England – Elizabeth never gave one of them a definite answer. She loved the elaborate wooing but she knew that almost any husband would bring disaster to the country. If he was an English or a Scottish lord, he would arouse the jealousy of the nobility; if he was French, Spain would declare war; a Catholic would infuriate the Protestants and a Protestant husband would provoke the Catholics to rebellion, so she continued to play the marriage game until she was an old woman. In her heart she probably never intended to marry anyone, unless it could have been Leicester, and she was too cool-headed to marry for love.

SEA CAPTAINS

MEANWHILE, in England's ports and seafaring towns, there was much talk of the riches which Portuguese and Spanish captains were bringing back from distant lands and Englishmen began to awake to a sense of what they were missing. In Edward VI's reign, old Sebastian Cabot was bribed to come home from Spain to advise on ocean voyages and it was Northumberland who sent out the first important expeditions since the discovery of Newfoundland. Because the Portuguese and the Spaniards had divided the New World between themselves, and the way to India was also barred by the Portuguese, Sebastian advised a voyage to the north-east, in the belief that there was a sea-route round northern Europe which could lead to India, Cathay and the Spice Islands.

Three ships commanded by Sir Hugh Willoughby set out from Greenwich but in the icy seas off Lapland, Willoughby and two of the ships were lost. Richard Chancellor brought the third vessel into a bay of northern Russia, known then as Muscovy, and, finding no way to the sunlit East, he resolutely made a one-thousand-mile journey by sledge to Moscow where he attended the

Court of the Great Tsar, Ivan the Terrible. A treaty was made and, although Chancellor perished on his next voyage, the Muscovy Company was set up to promote trade in furs, hides, tallow and cloth with a country which was almost totally unknown to the rest of Europe.

This modest success did not appeal greatly to those who dreamed of gold and spices. William Hawkins, a merchant shipbuilder of Plymouth, made several voyages to the coasts of West Africa where he annoyed the Portuguese by trading with the natives for gold-dust and ivory. Nearer home, English ships cruised about the Channel in order to rob Spanish vessels on their way to the Netherlands and when King Philip protested indignantly to Elizabeth, she replied that she simply did not know that her subjects were behaving so badly. She was well aware, however, that William Hawkins had built himself a private fleet from the profits of piracy and more lawful trade and that he would loyally use it in the Queen's service.

William's son, John Hawkins, extended the family business when he sailed to West Africa to buy or capture negroes in order to sell them to the planters in Spanish America. Philip forbade trade of any kind by foreigners in those waters but, by a mixture of charm and threats, Hawkins induced the planters to do business with him. No one thought there was anything wrong in selling slaves and the Spanish settlers could not grow sugar or work the silver mines without slave labour.

Twice, Hawkins came home with a good profit and, for his third voyage, the Queen contributed one of her own ships to his little fleet. Once again, he traded successfully along the Spanish Main and was about to return when a gale damaged his ships so severely that he was forced to enter the Spanish port of San Juan in the

Gulf of Mexico. Taken unawares, the Spaniards raised
no objections and work had begun on the damaged
vessels when a Spanish fleet was sighted approaching
the port. Hawkins had seized the harbour fort and it
would have been possible for him to keep the fleet out
but Spain and England were officially at peace and he
would get no thanks from his Queen for committing an
open act of war. So he decided to allow the Spanish ships
to come in and it was agreed that neither side should
molest the other.

Two days later, the Spaniards made a sudden attack,
killing all the English sailors ashore and opening fire on
Hawkins' fleet and boarding some of his ships. In a
furious hand-to-hand battle, the boarders were driven
off and, having ordered his cousin, Francis Drake, to
take the little *Judith* outside, Hawkins set about his
attackers so vigorously that he sank two galleons and
silenced the rest. Meanwhile, the Spanish shore-bat-
teries had reduced his flag-ship, the Queen's own vessel,
to a wreck, so he transferred most of the gold and silver
into the *Minion* and fought his way out of the harbour to
join the *Judith* at anchor for the night.

Next morning, for some reason never explained,
Drake had vanished, leaving his commander in the lurch
with a leaky ship containing two hundred men and very
few provisions. A hundred men volunteered to be put
ashore in the hope of surviving until a rescue ship could
reach them from England. In fact, some were killed by
Indians and the rest captured by the Spaniards. Years
later Hawkins managed to obtain the release of a few
survivors.

Meanwhile, the *Minion* made a nightmare voyage to
England and there were only fifteen starving men left
alive when Devon was sighted. Drake had already arrived and the news of the Spaniards' treachery rang

through England. From that day, there was undeclared war between English and Spanish seamen no matter where they chanced to meet.

While the Queen insisted upon keeping the methodical Hawkins at home to build the royal fleet, Drake made several voyages to the New World where, in revenge for San Juan, he plundered the Spanish settlements and attacked King Philip's ships without warning. During one of his shore expeditions on the Isthmus of Panama, a runaway slave showed him a giant tree with steps cut in its side. Ascending to a platform in the upper branches, Drake caught the first glimpse of the Pacific Ocean, which no Englishman had ever seen before:

'Almighty God,' he murmured, 'grant me life and leave to sail but once an English ship on that great sea.'

His prayer was granted when the 'Master Thief', as the Spaniards called Drake, sailed the *Golden Hind* into the Pacific and then, having robbed the Spaniards along the South American coast and claimed 'New Albion' (California) for the Queen, continued westward to the East Indies, the Cape of Good Hope and back to Plymouth Sound. This voyage round the world was important, not so much for the gold and spices aboard Drake's little ship or because he was knighted by the Queen on his own deck, but because he had inspired generations of Englishmen to set out in search of knowledge and adventure.

For the moment, the magnet that drew men to the New World was the treasure which the Spaniards wrung from the conquered peoples of Central America. In the sea-towns of Devonshire, ship after ship was fitted out, manned and victualled for the pirate trade of the Caribbean where they joined up with the other freebooters, mostly French and Dutch, to hunt down the Spanish

ships and to attack King Philip's treasure-houses
ashore.

Besides Drake, there were many others who were
urged on by greed for gold and by the excitement of
finding out more about a world which had recently
become so much wider than anyone had ever imagined.
They took risks and accepted their failures. Sir Richard
Grenville, one of the most rugged of gentlemen-adven-
turers, had a scheme to explore the southern seas and the
unknown continent that was supposed to lie there. This
came to nothing, but then Sir Humphrey Gilbert and Sir
Walter Raleigh proposed to start colonies in North America where Englishmen could build new homes and still
remain loyal subjects of the Queen. In Newfoundland
and Virginia, their schemes failed and Gilbert, on his

way home in the tiny *Squirrel*, was lost in mid-Atlantic.
Friends aboard an accompanying vessel caught a last
glimpse of him as the storm-driven ships came momen-
tarily close together; he was on deck 'with a book in his
hand, crying out to us ... "We are as near to Heaven by
sea as by land!" '

Martin Frobisher, a rougher sea-dog than the courtiers, explored the coasts of Greenland and Canada in
hope of finding a sea-passage to the East and he aroused
great excitement by bringing home some black stones
believed to contain gold. The Cathay Company was
formed to make fortunes for those who invested in ships
and smelting-furnaces, but when the stones proved to be
worthless poor Frobisher had difficulty in finding support for any other ventures. John Davis carried on the
Arctic explorations and, in the next reign, on yet
another voyage in search of the North-West Passage,
Henry Hudson was set adrift by a mutinous crew and
left to perish in those icy seas. The Passage did exist but
it was never to become the longed-for channel to the
riches of the East.

WAR WITH SPAIN

WHILE Drake was sailing round the world, war with Spain was becoming ever more certain. Elizabeth still tried to avoid an open conflict but Philip, exasperated by the impudence of her pirate-seamen, at last found himself in a better position to carry out his life's ambition to restore the Catholic religion in England and the Netherlands. France was no longer a danger to him and he had seized Portugal with all its wealth and shipping.

His Dutch subjects in the Netherlands had put up a most obstinate resistance but he intended to subdue them by the ferocity of the Duke of Parma's army. Near to collapse, the Dutch sent urgent appeals for more help to come out from England and Elizabeth was prevailed upon to send a small army under the command of Leicester, whose officers included his own nephew, Sir Philip Sidney.

This gifted young poet, beloved by everyone who met him, had been denied the chances of adventure by the Queen's fondness for him. She would keep her favourites at Court, giving them minor errands to carry out rather than allow them to risk their handsome necks on active service. However, once in the Netherlands, Sidney threw himself into the struggle with far more vigour than his uncle, and he had distinguished himself alongside the Dutch in several actions when the allies advanced to threaten the Spanish-held town of Zutphen. Parma dispatched supplies to his garrison and an English company was sent to intercept the food-convoy. Sidney joined the ambush-party at dawn; the supply-wagons were heard approaching when the mist lifted to reveal, not the usual light guard, but a heavy escort of musketeers and cavalry. Outnumbered by six to one, the English charged the convoy. Sidney's horse was killed and he had remounted and was back in the fight when a musket-ball, fired at close-range, smashed his thigh. In agony, he was taken back to Leicester's camp where men ran to assist him, one of them bringing water, and he was about to put his lips to the bottle when a soldier, horribly wounded in the same engagement, was carried by. Sidney saw the dying man's eyes light up with longing and he pushed the bottle towards him.

'Drink, thy necessity is yet greater than mine,' he said.

Sidney died later of his wound and the action at Zutphen was notable only because the English felt that it was there that they lost the noblest of all their young men. After this, the war went badly and the Dutch were harder pressed than ever. They got relief only when Philip finally lost patience with England.

The event that made Philip decide to overthrow
Elizabeth was the execution of Mary Queen of Scots.
Efforts to release her had been going on for years; plots
and a rising of northern Catholics had been punished
with a severity that would have made Henry VIII blink;
the Duke of Norfolk and others were beheaded and for
the first time in the reign, Catholics of all classes began
to suffer persecution. One day, an empty beer-barrel left
the castle in which Mary was a prisoner and in the bung

was a letter in which she apparently gave her consent to a plot to invade England and kill Elizabeth. The brewer's drayman, in the pay of both sides, handed the letter to the government's agent. It was enough. For years William Cecil, now Lord Burghley, had been begging the Queen to put an end to this constant danger and now, sharply supported by Parliament, he demanded that she should sign Mary's death warrant. Elizabeth yielded and two days later, in Fotheringay

Castle, Mary met her death with brave dignity. She left her claim to the English throne, not to her son James, but to Philip of Spain.

At once Philip began to plan the invasion. It was a long and costly business, for warships and troop carriers had to be built and other vessels were bought in various foreign harbours and taken to Spain to be fitted out. Stores, gunpowder, shot and armour had to be amassed in huge quantities, besides the crucifixes and holy banners which the priests would carry ashore. This great fleet, or Armada, would deal with any English warships in the Channel, but its prime purpose was to carry 20,000 men and stores to the Duke of Parma. Most of the front-line invasion army would be drawn from the Low Countries and it was Parma's task to bring his tough experienced troops to the coast and to construct the flat-bottomed barges that would carry them and their horses across the narrow sea to England.

Philip's immense preparations could not be kept secret and in England there was great activity in the shipyards and on the greens where men practised their weapons and drill. In a daring bid to delay the invasion, Drake sailed his fleet past the guns of Cadiz harbour to capture and destroy thirty-seven Spanish warships besides vast quantities of equipment. Philip ruefully made his losses good and in the summer of 1588 the great Armada set sail.

On 19th July the Cornish coast was sighted and the Spanish admiral, the Duke of Medina Sidonia, ordered the fleet to take up close formation, with his most powerful warships leading the way to protect the mass of troopships and store vessels. On either side and at the rear came more fighting ships to ward off attacks. Of the 130 vessels, about 50 were warships. The fleet moved very slowly under reduced canvas, for the wind was light and it was difficult to make the cumbersome troopships keep their positions.

The English had stationed Lord Seymour in the Downs to keep a watch out for Parma's barges but their main fleet lay at Plymouth under the command of Lord Howard, with Drake, Hawkins and Frobisher each commanding a squadron. Upon news of the Armada's arrival, they had some difficulty in getting to sea but by skilful use of the south-west wind, they sailed across the front of the Spaniards and worked up wind until they had the advantage and could begin to attack.

For a week, a confused battle took place in the Channel as the Armada held its course at a snail's pace and the English attacked along its edges. Three or four great galleons were disabled and many others were damaged, but the Spaniards' gunnery was better than Drake had expected and the English, getting desperately short of ammunition, had not succeeded in breaking the formation or causing havoc among the troopships when Medina Sidonia anchored off Calais. Word was sent ashore to Parma to ask what he proposed to do. In truth, he could do very little, for his troops and barges were still some miles further up the coast and the Armada's pilots were unwilling to venture into those shallow waters. The wind began to rise and the Spaniards, with no sizeable port in which they could shelter, found themselves in a precarious position.

In England, where Grenville and Raleigh commanded the West Country levies and the Queen put on armour and went down to Tilbury to address her army, there was every intention of giving the Spaniards a hot reception if they got ashore. Meanwhile Howard, lying at anchor a mile to windward of the enemy, had sent to Dover for fireships. When these failed to arrive, eight large merchantmen serving with the fleet were hurriedly got ready and at midnight, on a strong east-going tide, they were sent blazing into the crowded anchorage. In panic, most of the Spanish captains ordered the anchor cables to be cut and their ships drifted off into the darkness, colliding with one another as they tried to get out to sea. At dawn, the great fleet was scattered along the coast and the English were sailing into the attack.

All day they pounded the enemy and tried to drive him on to the sandbanks while the Spaniards fought desperately to edge out into the North Sea. Thousands of their men were killed or drowned and their ships were horribly damaged but only one was boarded and a few others were grounded or sunk. A gale came up and the battered Armada could only flee northwards pursued by the English more for show than anything, for they had long since run out of ammunition. Only fifty-three ships, fewer than half of the great Armada, ever came back to Spain where Medina Sidonia, who had done far better than most of his captains, was reviled by everyone except King Philip. 'I sent you out to war with men, not with the elements,' he said. Philip had no intention of giving up after one failure and, with infinite patience, he began to prepare another fleet.

The English, astonished by the completeness of the enemy's overthrow, celebrated the victory with processions, bonfires and merrymaking. Their leaders, especially Hawkins and Drake, were well aware that the destruction of a single fleet had not removed all the danger. Drake wished to attack the rest of King Philip's navy, while Hawkins vainly put forward his own plan of intercepting the treasure ships before they reached Spain.

The sequel to the Armada's defeat was less glorious. Drake's attack on Corunna failed and the Spaniards' use of fast well-armed ships for the Atlantic crossing, in

place of the old slow-moving galleons, enabled them to
evade the English sea-robbers. The Queen, always tight-
fisted over her Navy, became less inclined to spend
money on ships than on land operations in France, Ireland and the Netherlands.

Old Grenville, roaring defiance to the end, died of
wounds in the last fight of the *Revenge*. Frobisher was
killed in an attack on a Spanish stronghold and Drake
and Hawkins both died at sea during their last raid in
the West Indies. The expedition was mismanaged from
the start. The Spaniards knew that their old foes were

coming and the two commanders, never at ease with
each other since San Juan, could seldom agree.
Hawkins, worn out after a lifetime of service to the
Queen, could only think of her as he lay dying: 'Assure
Her Majesty of my love and loyalty,' he murmured, and
he left her £2,000 of his own money to make amends for
failing to win the Spaniards' treasure.

Drake also knew that he would never be given another
fleet if he returned empty-handed but there was nothing
to be had at San Juan, at Nombre de Dios or on the
Isthmus of Panama and he was still muttering, 'We must
have gold', when the greatest of Elizabeth's sea-captains
died at Porto Bello.

There was, however, one last triumph in the year of

Drake's death, just eight years after the Armada. Philip had amassed another great fleet at Cadiz when Howard, Raleigh and Essex sailed in, captured the town and destroyed the shipping. The Queen grumbled that they brought home too little booty but she was growing old and crotchety, and Philip himself was dying. Their long struggle was at its end.

THE GLORY OF HER REIGN

WITH the sense of peril gone, some of the sparkle went out of Elizabeth's reign. As danger receded, people had time to think about the difficulties at home and to voice complaints.

The new wealth which came from better methods of farming, from mining, cloth-making, manufacturing and sea-trading, was ill-divided. It flowed mostly into the pockets of the rich.

A feature of the reign was unemployment, something never known before in a country where for centuries every man's work, usually on the land, had been as necessary as the rain and the sunshine. But the population was growing; some men lost their strips of land or sold them cheap and drifted away to the towns; vagabonds swarmed the countryside and made the roads unsafe for travellers; London teemed with rogues and cutpurses and although Elizabeth's Poor Law made it the duty of every parish to look after its poor, there was still a host of men without work. In the capital, they became a rabble, living as best they could in shacks and hovels, surviving only by odd jobs, begging and crime.

As some went down, others rose in the world. Yeomen, farmers and merchants joined the ranks of the gentry who were now becoming more important than the nobles, and as the gentry realized their power, they wanted a greater share in the government. They regarded the old Queen with awe not far removed from worship but in the House of Commons they began to question her right to decide all things with her own ministers. From time to time, they dared to draw her attention to some pressing matter or even to hold up her 'supplies' or taxes and she treated them with disdain or anger or gracious courtesy, according to her mood. They loved her and she knew it and took advantage of them

but they were growing restive and the day would come
when, instead of beseeching the monarch's will, they
would demand their rights.

In the Commons, as in the towns and some country
districts, the Puritans were growing in numbers and
influence. Their strict way of life, their hatred of the
Roman Catholics and disgust at Elizabeth's religious
settlement appealed to some of the gentry and to many
of the merchants and tradespeople who as aldermen and
councillors ruled the towns. For her part, she detested
them and did all she could to reduce their influence.

Thus, as she grew old, Elizabeth's triumphs and
achievements were clouded by difficulties. Yet nothing
could dim the glory of her reign. Englishmen had found
a new pride and confidence in themselves. They rejoiced

in their sailors, their growing trade, their new houses and all the signs of mounting prosperity in a bustling, adventurous age. New ideas and knowledge came flooding into the country, though Elizabeth's people, eager, quarrelsome and reckless, saw nothing to envy in what they knew of foreign places. To them, their capital with its splendid waterfront, their little towns fiercely claiming the right to a market and a mayor, their lovely countryside and, above all, their own freedom to say what they liked or to die saying it, seemed beyond compare. They were a young people with a matchless Queen and a score of heroes who could write poetry, storm a fortress or plant a colony beyond the seas.

But the greatest genius of the Elizabethan age was neither a courtier nor a man of action. He was the son of a Warwickshire corn merchant and glove-maker.

John Shakespeare, one-time alderman, town bailiff and man of business, fell into debt and disgrace and there were those who hinted that his son Will would speedily go the same way. The boy had no liking for steady employment but was forever idling his time on the green or at the inn, playing the fool to other idlers by imitating the strolling players who from time to time visited the town. When he was older and had hardly a penny to his hame, he married a farmer's daughter, but odd jobs and a bit of poaching were not enough to keep a family on, so Anne and her babies went back to her father's farm and Will Shakespeare left Stratford-on-Avon to seek his fortune in London.

The capital was full of country lads who had come on the same errand and Shakespeare found life as hard as the rest. His ambition to be an actor was lowly enough, at a time when actors were looked upon as hardly better than vagabonds. However, he managed to attract the attention of James Burbage, owner of one of London's two theatres, who allowed him to make himself useful and presently to take some small acting parts. It was ill-paid work and there was little enough money to send home to Stratford until the company discovered that Will had more ability for writing than for acting. Mostly, they had to rely on stories and legends into which they inserted popular happenings and pieces of tomfoolery to amuse the crowd, but now they had found a man with a gift not merely for polishing up the old tales but for writing new plays with a host of characters who held the audiences spellbound. Nothing like these plays had ever been seen before and Shakespeare's company began to thrive so mightily that he and his friend, Richard Burbage, decided to build a new theatre at Bankside.

Courtiers, merchants, shopkeepers and apprentice-boys flocked across the river to the *Globe* where, seated in the galleries or standing in the open pit, they cheered and wept at the first performances of Shakespeare's plays. The ne'er-do-well from Stratford made a comfortable little fortune, enough to buy a fine house in his home town and to pay off his father's debts. During the next reign, he himself retired there to his garden with its mulberry tree, and when he died he was buried in the chancel of his parish church.

The great Queen fell ill in March 1603 but would neither go to bed nor take medicine. She was tired and lonely, for her old friends and enemies were dead and she was saddened by the rebellion of her last favourite, the foolish, handsome Essex whom she had sent to the executioner's block. Only when her own end was very near would she name her succesor: 'I will that a king succeed me, and who but my kinsman the King of Scots?'

It was 24th March, 1603, and Sir Robert Carey set out to ride full speed to Edinburgh with the news that Elizabeth was dead and James VI of Scotland was King of England.

JAMES OF SCOTLAND AND ENGLAND

JAMES, the only child of Mary Queen of Scots and Darnley, was a delicate boy who could not stand without help until he was seven. In later life, he always leaned on the arm of an attendant, and when riding he had to be strapped to the saddle, though he was a keen and reckless huntsman. As a boy he was uncommonly clever at his lessons, and his guardians made sure that he had the best and sternest tutor who did not hesitate to birch him if his answers were less than perfect.

This timid, lonely child was merely a puppet in the hands of his violent nobles, but when he grew up he managed to subdue them by trickery and by playing one off against another. He survived all his difficulties and ruled Scotland a good deal better than most of his ancestors and he took care to do nothing to offend his cousin Elizabeth. He was determined not to lose his chance of inheriting England's wealth and even when his mother was sentenced to death, he secretly assured Elizabeth that his threats of invasion meant nothing at all. Sixteen years later, when Carey brought the joyful news, he lost little time in setting out for London. His patience had been rewarded. Without the loss of a single life, he had reached the throne which all the power of Spain and France had failed to win.

The English accepted their new monarch quietly, though his appearance and manners did nothing to arouse their enthusiasm. His clothes were shabby, he seldom washed and, apart from being lame, he spoke in the oddest fashion, spluttering and lolling out his tongue

as though it were too big for his mouth. Moreover, although his conversation was often full of good sense and
humour, he gave the impression that he thought himself
so clever that everyone else was a fool. And, having come
into a fortune, he lavished enormous gifts upon the
rowdy favourites who accompanied him and he made it
clear that he much preferred Scotsmen to English courtiers.

There were nevertheless a good many who welcomed
his coming. Both the Puritans and Catholics hoped that
James would be kind to their religion but he soon disappointed them. At Hampton Court, he treated a gathering of Puritan clergymen with great rudeness and ended
by losing his temper and shouting that if they did not
obey the rules of the Church of England, he would harry

them out of the kingdom. As for the Catholics, he showed them much more politeness at first but, finding that this alarmed Parliament, he allowed them to be persecuted by heavy fines and the banishment of their priests.

In desperation, a handful of Catholic hot-heads made a plot to kill the King and the leading men of the country when they assembled for the opening of Parliament. The conspirators, Robert Catesby, Thomas Percy and others, obtained the services of Guy Fawkes, a Yorkshireman serving in Flanders with the Spanish army, who was brought over to act as their explosives expert. A start was made by digging a tunnel from a cellar next to Parliament House but this was abandoned when Fawkes discovered that they could hire a large storeroom right underneath the House of Lords. Into this room he managed to take thirty-six barrels of gunpowder which he covered over with coals, firewood and bars of iron.

Leaving Fawkes as sentinal, the rest of the conspirators dispersed in order to collect arms and horses but among those in on the secret was a man who did not wish to kill his kinsman Lord Monteagle. He therefore sent him a note, advising him not to attend the opening of Parliament but 'to retire into the country ... for ... they shall receive a terrible blow'.

The letter was passed to the council and on 4th November, 1605, the Lord Chamberlain made a tour of inspection. When he looked into the lumber-room and inquired who owned the fuel, Fawkes coolly replied that it belonged to his master, a gentleman named Percy. This name excited suspicion but when, late at night, a party of soldiers arrived, Fawkes was still at his post, doubtless hoping that courage and bluff would see him through. Arrested and taken before the King he did not deny his intention but, turning fiercely to the Scottish courtiers, declared that one of his objects was 'to blow the Scots back to Scotland!' Under torture, he refused to give the names of any of the plotters until he learned that they had died at bay in a Staffordshire country-house. Then, so maimed that he could not walk to the gallows, he went bravely to his death.

The Gunpowder Plot ruined the Catholic cause in England, but instead of taking advantage of the situation, James I speedily fell out with Parliament. In conversation and in a book which he wrote, he put forward the notion of Divine Right, declaring that since a king was appointed by God, he could make or break his subjects 'like men at chess'. They must always obey and their so-called rights and privileges were merely gifts from the King.

This kind of talk might have been all very well coming from Henry VIII but it would not do for Englishmen who, having beaten the Spaniards and overcome so many dangers, were in no mood to surrender their rights to a threadbare Scot. Their one check on the King was the ancient right to vote him the customs duties but when, instead of meekly doing so, they insisted on talking about their grievances, James dismissed them and ruled for ten years without Parliament.

By raising money in various ways, James could just manage as long as he did not have to pay for a war, and his policy, therefore, was to make friends with both the Catholics and Protestants abroad. He married his beautiful daughter Elizabeth to the leading Protestant Prince (or Elector) of Germany and he also made peace with Spain.

THE FIRST COLONIES

THE peace displeased those who looked on war with the Spaniards as a religious duty and a nice source of plunder. The most vigorous enemy of Spain was Sir Walter Raleigh, one of Elizabeth's favourites who had founded the colony of Virginia in her honour, had organized various expeditions against the Spaniards and had made a voyage to Central America where he believed he had only narrowly missed discovering El Dorado, the fabulous land of gold. However, early in the reign, Raleigh was arrested on a charge of treason and sent to the Tower where he spent the next thirteen years writing a history of the world and petitioning the King for his release. In return for freedom, he promised to bring him the gold of El Dorado.

While he was in prison, one of Raleigh's many schemes did get under way. His original colony in Virginia had failed, but in 1607 another party of settlers was sent out to America where they built a settlement named James Town. As in the past, it was not long before they were in dire straits. Many of the settlers were down-at-heel gentlemen, servants and petty tradesmen who had come out in hopes of an easy life, not to work hard felling trees and ploughing the soil. Bad leadership, perpetual quarrelling and semi-starvation almost destroyed them in the first year. One man saved the colony.

Even in an age of adventure, Captain John Smith's career was remarkable. A farmer's son, orphaned in boyhood, he had run away from his guardian, had fought the Spaniards in the Netherlands, had served as gunner on a French pirate-ship and had joined the Imperial Army to fight against the Turks in Hungary. Thanks to his cunning and bravery, he rose to the rank of captain but, left for dead on a battlefield, he was taken prisoner and forced to work as a slave in Turkey and afterwards in southern Russia. Thence he escaped across the steppes to Poland and reached England penniless but still thirsting for fresh adventures. Having joined the colonists, Smith quickly sized up the ne'er-do-wells and made no secret of his contempt for their indolence while they, for their part, detested him and did their utmost to have him hanged.

Only when the colony was on the verge of starvation did the grumblers accept Smith as leader and he at once introduced discipline and regular work into the settlement. Unfortunately, on an expedition up-country, he was captured by the Red Indians and taken before the Great Chief whom he impressed by his courage and godlike wisdom. But the Chief, rightly believing that white men were his mortal enemies, nevertheless ordered him to be put to death. His life was saved by the little Princess Pocahontas who flung herself between the brave captain and the warriors who were about to dash his brains out.

Having contrived to return to the settlement where only thirty-eight men were still alive, Smith again restored its fortunes until, with fresh shiploads of settlers

arriving every year, the colony began to prosper. Farms were established, tobacco (despite King James's opposition) became a profitable crop and, in increasing numbers, Englishmen came out to make their homes in North America.

The most celebrated of all the expeditions to Virginia never arrived there. In 1620, a party of Puritans, known as Separatists, who had already tried to settle in Holland, left England in a ship called the *Mayflower* in order to found a settlement in Virginia where they might worship God in their own fashion. One hundred and two 'Pilgrims', as they called themselves, were crowded below decks in the little ship and they had to endure the horrors of an Atlantic voyage during the autumn gales. After ten weeks at sea the battered *Mayflower* dropped anchor near Cape Cod, and the pilgrims found that they had been driven hundreds of miles to the north of Virginia. Naming the land New England, they decided to go ashore rather than endure life at sea any longer. A settlement called New Plymouth was started and, under their leaders, William Bradford, John Carver and a stout little captain named Miles Standish, the colonists settled down to face their first winter. When spring came, barely half the company was still alive, for hunger, intense cold and attacks by Indians had carried off all but the strongest.

Unlike John Smith's party, the 'Pilgrim Fathers' were ready to work and to live in harmony. By intense labour, these steadfast men and women managed to support themselves and to raise crops so that at the end of the summer, when the harvest was in, they held a feast of thankfulness for God's mercies and this is still kept as a holiday called Thanksgiving Day in America. After this, the colony grew steadily, as the Indians were pushed back and new towns and villages were built.

Two years before the *Mayflower* sailed, Raleigh himself was dead. Shortage of money had prompted James to let him out of the Tower in order to fetch the gold from El Dorado. On no account must he molest the Spaniards. This was really an impossible condition for, even if the gold existed, it was absurd to believe that the Spaniards would tamely allow a party of Englishmen to carry it away. James probably hoped that if the expedition succeeded, he could pretend he knew nothing about it.

Overjoyed at his release, Raleigh collected a fleet of fourteen ships and set out for Guiana where the Spaniards, warned of his coming, were already on the alert. By the time the mouth of the Orinoco River was reached, Raleigh's health, ruined by long imprisonment, had broken down and he was too ill to accompany the exploring party which proceeded up-river in boats and pinnaces. He remained aboard ship and was still in his cabin when an exhausted survivor returned with a tale of disaster. Having gone ashore, the Englishmen had attacked a Spanish fort guarding the route inland and had been repulsed with heavy losses, including Raleigh's own son. The expedition was a complete failure and there was nothing left but to return home.

Raleigh made no attempt to escape punishment. The Spaniards were demanding his head and after King James had considered handing him over to them for trial, he decided instead that the death sentence passed years before should be carried out.

Ill, and disappointed in all his grand hopes, Raleigh met his end with cheerful courage, remarking to the bystanders at the scaffold, 'I have a long journey to make and I must bid the company farewell,' and then, running his thumb along the axe's edge, added, 'Here is a sure cure for all diseases!'

But if Raleigh's death was meant to please the Spaniards, the royal marriage plan only led to worse ill-feeling than ever. Prince Charles and his friend Villiers, the Duke of Buckingham, made a secret trip to woo the Spanish Princess in her own country, but the foolish pair behaved with such conceited arrogance that the Spaniards declared they would rather throw their Princess down a well than see her married to such a fellow. So, having made themselves the laughing-stock of Europe, the silly young men came home without the lady.

James's hopes for the Protestant alliance failed just as dismally. His daughter and her husband became King and Queen of Bohemia but the Catholics drove them out within a year and Elizabeth, known as the 'Winter Queen' from the shortness of her reign, went to live in exile in Holland where, penniless but gay, she held court to her admirers and raised a large family, including a headstrong lad named Rupert.

James died in 1625, leaving the kingdom much weaker than when he had come to England twenty-two years previously. Not all his difficulties were his own fault. Many of them went back to Elizabeth's time – the shortage of money, Parliament's demands to have a bigger say in the government, the rising influence of the Puritans and the widespread feeling that the Church of England was too much like the Church of Rome. But whereas Elizabeth had been able to manage her people and parliaments, James lacked her dignity and tact. He had no charm and he never knew when to yield gracefully. Worse still, he was never successful at anything. War with Spain had started again, the fleet and the army were hopelessly weak and Parliament trusted neither the King nor his ministers.

CHARLES I

THE son to whom James left these difficulties was a much more attractive man than his father. Charles I looked like a king. Handsome, with a noble air of dignity, he was also kind and generous, a good husband and lover of beautiful pictures and artistic treasures. Regarding himself as a man of honour, he honestly believed that he conducted himself like a Christian gentleman, and he never understood that beneath his good qualities he had faults that were to bring him to ruin.

Charles had been brought up to believe in the Divine Right of Kings. Since God had made him a king, he was above the laws which common mortals had to obey and this allowed him to break promises and to deceive even his own friends. He lacked the power to make sharp decisions and had a genius for taking bad advice. Worst of all, his love of double-dealing made it impossible for anyone to trust him.

The reign opened badly. Buckingham, whom Charles adored, speedily arranged for him to marry Henrietta Maria, the King of France's fifteen-year-old sister. This annoyed the mainly Protestant Parliament which did not relish the prospect of a Catholic Queen bringing up her children in her own religion and, in any case, it would have been difficult to find a more unsuitable wife for Charles. Henrietta Maria was a pretty, feather-headed girl who grew into an obstinate woman, devoted to her husband but forever plaguing him with reckless advice to ignore Parliament and to rule as he pleased.

The war with Spain was disastrous. Buckingham shipped an army of hastily raised troops to Holland where the 'raw and poor rascals' mostly perished of hunger and disease. A naval attack on Cadiz with rotten ships, some not refitted since the Armada, was a complete fiasco and then, as though in love with failure, Buckingham decided to make war on France! He had led an ill-equipped expedition to defeat at La Rochelle and was preparing further disasters, when an assassin killed him at Portsmouth.

By this time, Charles was on the worst possible terms with Parliament. Three times he sent them home when he found that the members, instead of granting him taxes, wanted to bring his friend Buckingham to trial. To obtain money for the war, he demanded 'forced loans' from every county and imprisoned a number of the gentry who refused to pay. Parts of the country were placed under military law, men were seized for the army and soldiers were billeted upon householders without pay.

Charles was soon in such straits for money that he had to call Parliament and accept the Petition of Right, which declared the Englishman's right to be free from this kind of tyranny. But a King who believed in Divine Right did not feel obliged to keep promises and having brought the war to an end, he decided to rule without interference from a parliament.

For eleven years he managed to do so. The government muddled along on the money that could be raised by one means or another. Ship Money, a wartime tax paid in counties close to the sea, was demanded from all the counties and this aroused much indignation since it had not been passed by Parliament. John Hampden, a Buckinghamshire squire, refused to pay. The King's judges decided against him but he escaped arrest and was later to die fighting on Parliament's side. His example encouraged others to resist the royal tyranny.

Charles's chief ministers were now Sir Thomas Wentworth and William Laud, Archbishop of Canterbury. Wentworth believed in strong government and, as President of the Council in the north of England, he managed affairs with great efficiency, caring nothing for private persons but only for the good of the state. Made Earl of Strafford, he went to rule Ireland by the same stern system, which he called 'Thorough', and brought that turbulent country to a state of order it had not known for centuries. Wentworth's success made a deep impression on the King's opponents. They dreaded to think that 'Black Tom Tyrant', as they called him, might come to rule England in the same way.

If Strafford was feared, Archbishop Laud was hated. This sharp-tongued little man reformed the Church of England, inspected its parishes, punished the clergy for their errors and did his utmost to crush the puritans by fines, imprisonment and penalties such as the cutting-off of ears.

Not content with wanting to make everyone in England worship in the same way, Charles and Laud rashly tried to do the same in Scotland. But most of the Lowland Scots were strong Presbyterians who believed in long sermons and plain services. Robes, ceremony and anything that reminded them of Catholic forms of worship filled them with horror. This did not please Laud and he ordered all Scottish churches to start using an English Prayer Book on a certain Sunday in 1637.

The cathedral of St Giles in Edinburgh was crowded when the Dean, wearing a white robe instead of the usual black, began to read the new prayers to his stern-faced congregation. He had not gone far when an old woman named Jenny Geddes, unable to bear what she believed to be the words of a Catholic service, started up, crying, 'Thou false thief, wilt thou say Mass at my ear?' Snatching hold of her stool, she hurled it at the Dean's head, whereupon uproar broke out in the cathedral, with people shouting, 'The Mass! The Mass! Down with Popery!' whilst others tore off the Dean's white surplice and well-nigh killed him. The Bishop himself was in danger until soldiers were called in to clear the church and restore order.

After this, all southern Scotland was up in arms. Thousands signed a document called the Covenant, binding themselves to fight for their form of religion, and Charles was forced to withdraw the hated Prayer Book. With his usual obstinacy, he would not leave the matter there. He decided to make the Scots obey by force of arms but, although he sent for Strafford to come over from Ireland, his unwilling conscripts, many of them Puritan lads, were no match for the determined Scots. In the Bishops' War, the Scots marched across the border, captured Newcastle and refused to go home until they were paid to do so. Having no money, Charles was forced to summon a parliament.

The Long Parliament, so called because it lasted for many years, assembled in 1640. Led by Hampden and John Pym, the members came to Westminster determined to make the King rule according to custom and law, and they were also set upon putting an end to Strafford.

'Black Tom' was about to train a royal army in the north, but he came to London at the King's request and advised him to arrest his opponents in Parliament. He himself went boldly to the House of Lords to hear an accusation of high treason which had been raised against him. 'I will go and look my accusers in the face!' he said contemptuously.

When the Commons found that they could not prove

treason, they passed a Bill of Attainder, an old way of getting rid of an opponent by simply declaring he was worthy of death. But the Bill required the King's consent and Strafford, although lodged in the Tower, was certain that Charles would not allow him to be harmed. He had said so in a letter. Pym therefore took charge. His agents spread rumours of an attack on London, a mob was encouraged to surround the royal palace at Whitehall, where, rioting and howling for Strafford's death all day and night, they broke the King's nerve. With no soldiers for protection, terrified for his family's safety and upset by his tearful hysterical wife, he gave in and signed the death warrant.

At first Strafford could not believe that the King had betrayed him. Then he rose and said bitterly, 'Put not

T–E

your trust in Princes.' Three days later, Archbishop Laud, also in the Tower, thrust his hands through the grating of his cell door in order to bless Strafford as he passed by on his way to the scaffold. When the axe fell, the mob burst out in frenzied joy, 'His head is off! Black Tom! His head is off!'

After this, the situation grew worse. The King agreed to all Parliament's demands but he was also looking round for support wherever he might find it. A Royalist party known as the Cavaliers began to arm; street-mobs egged on by Puritan preachers, chanted, 'No bishops!' and Pym drew up an insulting list of the King's faults.

Suddenly, Charles made up his mind to act. He would arrest the leaders of the House of Commons, but instead of doing so at once, he let the House of Lords know what he intended and it was not until the following day that he went to Westminster with 400 armed Cavaliers.

Having seated himself in the Speaker's chair, he called out the names of five members whom he regarded as his chief enemies. There was no reply. Pym, Hampden and three others had already slipped away to safety.

'Mr. Speaker, where are those five members whose names I have called?' demanded the King.

The Speaker fell upon his knees:

'Your Majesty,' he replied, 'I have neither eyes to see nor tongue to speak in this place but as the House may direct me.'

' 'Tis no matter,' said Charles. 'I think my eyes are as good as another's. All my birds have flown.'

Three days later, the royal family left London. While the King moved to York to raise an army, the Queen went abroad to pawn her jewels to buy arms and to try, with little success, to enlist support from foreign monarchs.

Parliament also made preparations for war. Pym engaged Philip Skippon, a professional soldier, to drill the citizen forces known as the Train Bands. Efforts were made to raise troops of cavalry, and in the country men like Hampden and Oliver Cromwell, a Huntingdonshire squire, began to train their tenants and the Puritan yeomen.

The first battle of the Civil War took place at Edgehill in the centre of England. Parliament's general, the Puritan Earl of Essex, advanced from London, but his cavalry was swept away by Prince Rupert, a tempestuous young giant who had fought in Germany and had come over to fight for his uncle, the King. While the Royalist horsemen gleefully pursued the enemy across country, a desperate struggle was waged on the field where Lord Lindsay, the King's commander, was killed and the Royal Standard was captured with Sir Edmund Verney's severed hand still clutching its pole. Just in time to save the day, Rupert returned with as many cavalry as he had been able to round up. Neither side had won but both claimed the victory and Essex sent urgent messages to Pym that London was in danger.

Rupert was all for dashing on to seize the capital before its defences had been put in order. With London taken, the war was as good as won. But Charles hesitated. He did not want any more bloodshed and his senior officers had already taken a strong dislike to Rupert's fiery contempt for their amateur soldiering. They advised caution and Charles moved away to Oxford where he set up his headquarters.

By the time the royal army advanced on London, Parliament's troops were barring the roads into the city. Entrenched in gardens and orchards where cavalry were useless, they put up so hot a resistance at Turnham Green that the Cavaliers retired to Oxford. However, for the next two years Charles seemed certain to win. Almost all the country districts, the west, all of Wales and the north were on his side. Most (but not all) of the gentry came to serve him, bringing their sons and tenant-farmers, with good horses and all the money they could scrape together.

The Royalist cavalry outclassed all opposition and Rupert, hardly ever out of the saddle, was the despair of Parliament's leaders. They never knew where he would appear next, raising troops, setting up strong-points and winning cavalry engagements whenever he came across the enemy. When he and his brother Maurice captured Bristol, Parliament's defeat seemed only a matter of time. Its army was weak, especially in cavalry which Cromwell contemptuously described as 'base and mean fellows ... old decayed serving-men and tapsters' – and the Puritan squire went back to East Anglia to train a force of psalm-singing Puritans, men who feared God and would fight, not for plunder, but for religion and liberty.

Pym sent to the Scots for help; Plymouth, Gloucester and Hull held firm and the tide of Royalist victories was checked. In truth, Parliament had the strength to win a long war, for London and most of the towns, with all their money and trade, were opposed to the King. So were the seaports and the navy, which made it difficult for Charles to obtain foreign help. As a result, he was always short of money, ammunition and reliable infantry.

Thus, after his early successes, the King's fortunes went downhill. Surrounded by scheming courtiers and quarrelsome generals, he never seemed able to take firm control or to find a strong man like Strafford to overawe the others. His friend Digby gave him nothing but bad advice and Rupert was too young and hot-headed to be supreme commander of the King's scattered forces.

In two great battles the war was lost. At Marston Moor, the Scots and Cromwell's new cavalry were too much for Rupert and, at Naseby, Fairfax and Cromwell destroyed the King's infantry. After this defeat Charles could only wander aimlessly about with the remnant of an army. His last hope lay in Scotland. Here the valiant Marquis of Montrose had raised the Highlanders and in a most brilliant campaign had defeated the Covenanters and had taken Glasgow and Edinburgh. In response to the King's despairing pleas, he tried to persuade the Lowlanders to join him in a march into England but the clansmen were defeated, and when he learned that Charles had given himself up to a Scottish army in Nottinghamshire, Montrose sorrowfully went to join the Queen in exile.

Rather than be captured by the Parliament men, Charles surrendered to the Scots. He thought they

would treat him more kindly and he had hopes of winning them over altogether. But the Scots wanted their
Presbyterian religion to be made the official religion of
England, and when Charles would not agree they
handed him over to Parliament.

Pym and Hampden were dead but it seemed clear
that Parliament had won. The King was a prisoner at
Holmby House and all that was needed was to make sure
that he would rule properly after the army had been sent
home. But the army would not go home. Their pay was
much overdue and they were not sure that Parliament
would favour the Puritan faith for which they had

fought. So they appealed to Cromwell who cut through all the arguments by sending a troop of horse to bring the King to the army headquarters.

Charles went willingly and was soon lodged comfortably at Hampton Court. He was highly amused by the turn things had taken. With Parliament, the army and the Scots all at loggerheads, he felt sure that he would triumph: 'When rogues fall out, honest men come into their own,' he remarked. Thus he refused the army's generous terms on which he could have regained his throne. Instead, he haggled and argued and then astonished everyone by escaping to the Isle of Wight where he took refuge in Carisbrooke Castle.

As usual, he miscalculated. The governor was not a Royalist after all and kept his guest in close confinement. By this time, however, Charles was in touch with the Scots, promising to establish their religion if they would come to the rescue and overthrow the army. Cromwell was furious. In a short campaign his Ironsides defeated the Scots and he was then master of the situation.

He dealt with Parliament by sending Colonel Pride to surround the House with soldiers. As each member arrived, he was seized and turned away unless he supported Cromwell and the army leaders. After Pride's Purge, only about fifty members of the Long Parliament were left and it was now nicknamed the Rump Parliament since it was only the tail-end of one. But what was to be done with the King, 'Charles Stuart, that man of blood', as the Puritans called him? All faith in his word had gone. Only anger remained. The Rump Parliament did as it was told and voted to have the King put on trial for high treason.

Scarcely half of the one hundred judges who were called to Westminster Hall came to the trial. Charles refused to acknowledge the court or to answer any of the charges against him. He had ruled badly, not because he had meant to be a despot, but because he obstinately believed that as King he could do no wrong. Now, accused of terrible crimes and in peril of his life, he faced his enemies with the utmost dignity.

The court found him guilty of being a tyrant, traitor, murderer and public enemy and he was brought from St James's Palace through heavily guarded streets to Whitehall where a scaffold was erected outside the Banqueting Hall.

The people of London, and in the rest of the country, were horrified by the sentence but they had no leaders and the Royalists were weak and scattered. The army was in command and although Fairfax was opposed to execution, Cromwell was grimly determined.

On 30th January, 1649, Charles stepped on to the scaffold, looked towards the great crowd kept back by close ranks of soldiers and with calm deliberation knelt down at the block. When the executioner held up his severed head, a great groan burst from the crowd, 'such a groan', wrote an eye-witness, 'as I never heard before and desire I may never hear again'.

OLIVER CROMWELL

AFTER the execution, it was decreed that England should have no more kings. The House of Lords was done away with, all men were to be equal and the government was to be called a Commonwealth. But many people were outraged by the King's death. The Scots and Irish were particularly angry and in Ireland a rebellion broke out against the English government.

Cromwell therefore took the New Model Army to Dublin. He and his soldiers detested the Catholic religion and had not forgotten the massacre of Protestants during the previous Irish rebellion. With merciless severity Cromwell subdued the country, killing the priests, putting prisoners to the sword and transporting thousands more overseas. Catholics were deprived of their estates and the unhappy people were left to their poverty and despair. In Ireland, the name of Cromwell is still cursed.

Certain that he had only done his duty, Cromwell returned to deal with the Scots who had proclaimed the King's son Charles II. Montrose, who had come over from Holland, had already been captured and executed when Cromwell won a crushing victory at Dunbar, but young Charles still managed to slip away over the border, in the hope of raising the English Royalists. But they did not flock to join the Prince as he expected. They disliked the Scots and feared the Ironsides, so when Cromwell caught up with Charles at Worcester, his experienced army made short work of the Royalist troops.

With a handful of his officers, young Charles escaped from the battlefield and took refuge in the woods where an impoverished family of loyalists gave him shelter. With Cromwell's men scouring the countryside, it would have been folly to try to escape with a troop of horsemen, so the King's clothes were exchanged for a labourer's breeches and doublet, his face was daubed with soot and his long curls hacked off with a pair of shears. Thus disguised, he hid in thickets and barns, made an attempt by night to cross the Severn into Wales, and trudged on torn and bleeding feet to Boscobel House where, with a Royalist officer, he was obliged to perch for hours in a huge oak tree from whose branches he could hear Cromwellian troopers discussing the reward for 'Charles Stuart, a long dark man, above two yards high'.

After this, loyal friends moved him about from one house to another, often by night but presently by day when, dressed now as a serving-man to a colonel's sister, he rode to Bristol, failed to find a ship there and retraced his steps across southern England. By luck and his own cheerful presence of mind, he and his friends survived one narrow squeak after another. There were times when he had to pass close to a troop of Parliament's soldiers, to lie hid in the priest-hole of a Catholic home or in an upper room of a house where the servants were untrustworthy.

In one place his food had to be hoisted to him by rope and pulley in the chimney, and at another an old servant came to him, fell on his knees and confessed that he knew who he was. Indeed, the royal fugitive was recognized by dozens of persons but most were ready to risk their lives to help him, and the sharp-eyed ostler who reported his suspicions to the local military commander was just too late. Charles and his friends had left the inn and, taking a wrong turning, were soon lost in the darkness!

At last the skipper of a coal-brig was found who was willing to take two cavalier gentlemen across to France, and just six weeks after the Battle of Worcester the tattered figure of the King of England waded ashore on the coast of Normandy.

Meanwhile, 'our chief of men', as the Puritans called Cromwell, had become all-powerful. The plain-spoken countryman was a natural leader and it seemed to him that God had chosen him to take command. What he wanted was an England governed by justice and Godliness but the men of the Rump Parliament were interested only in keeping their own power. For the moment, he did not disturb them because there was much to do.

An efficient navy had to be got to sea to tackle the Royalist fleet with which Rupert was carrying on the war. In Robert Blake, a soldier with little experience of the sea, Cromwell found one of England's finest admirals, and after Blake had dispersed Rupert's ships, war broke out with Holland. The two countries were rivals in trade and there was ill-feeling because the Dutch would not recognize England's new government. Their admiral van Tromp hoisted a broom to his mast-head to show that he had swept the English from the seas. But although Cromwell hated fighting against fellow-Protestants he had no intention of allowing his country to be defeated. A new fleet was fitted out and in a series of great battles, in which there were sometimes as many as 100 ships on either side, Blake and General Monk, another soldier-admiral, got the better of the Dutch and checked their sea power for the time being.

By now, Cromwell was thoroughly sick of the Rump Parliament. It was governing badly and still refused to put an end to its own existence, so, leaving a force of soldiers outside, he entered the House and sat for a while in his usual place, listening to the debate. Presently, he

rose and began to speak of the wrong things Parliament had done. Pointing an accusing finger at one member after another, he reminded them of their sins and petty acts of meanness. His anger almost choked him. Suddenly clapping his hat upon his head to show that he held them in no respect, he burst out:

'It is not right that you should sit as a Parliament any longer. You have sat long enough!'

A member rose to protest. This was the last straw to Cromwell.

'I will put an end to your prating!' he shouted. 'You are no Parliament. I say you are no Parliament.'

Turning to a friend, he added, 'Call them in! Call them in!' Thirty musketeers marched into the chamber and hustled the members out, as Cromwell continued to hurl reproaches at them for their evil ways. His eye fell

upon the Mace, symbol of the Speaker's authority. 'What are we to do with this bauble?' he asked one of the musketeers. 'Take it away!'

The doors of the House of Commons were locked and there was no government in the land except the stern commander-in-chief of Britain's armies. He still wanted a good Parliament at Westminster but if he allowed free elections, the voters would undoubtedly choose a Royalist Parliament. So the Army Council of Officers did the choosing and put forward the names of 150 God-fearing persons, the first of whom was called Praise-God Barebone. But Barebone's Parliament had no notion of how to govern and its members soon agreed to abandon the task. At this, the army invited Cromwell to rule as Lord Protector.

For the first time in over half a century, England's name was respected on the Continent. Peace was signed with the Dutch, alliances and trade agreements were made with the Protestant countries. Spain, still hostile, refused to allow free trade in the West Indies and persisted in capturing and persecuting English sailors whenever possible. When war broke out, Cromwell's power was plain to see, for the English fleet captured the rich sugar-island of Jamaica, intercepted the treasure-ships and sank sixteen galleons at Santa Cruz. On land, the New Model Army showed their fighting qualities in Flanders where they beat a Spanish army and captured the frontier town of Dunkirk.

Great as they were, these triumphs did not make the Lord Protector happy. He tried his best to give the people good government with freedom of worship for all except the Catholics, but there was so much argument and discontent that he found himself becoming more of a tyrant than Charles I had ever tried to be. He dismissed judges who failed to support him, imposed heavy taxes to pay for the wars and when murmurings grew louder, he divided the country into districts under Military Law. His power depended not upon the laws of the land and the people's goodwill but solely upon the swords and muskets of his soldiers, and since the major-generals who ruled the local districts were strict Puritans, all kinds of harmless pleasures and sports were forbidden.

The people hated Cromwell's rule but they feared him too much to attempt to overthrow him. Power brought him no contentment but deep sorrow and the fear of assassination. Only in his family and his horses did he find happiness, and the death of his favourite daughter broke his heart. After ruling the country almost single-handed for nine years, he died at Whitehall, worn out by the difficulties of the task which he had taken upon himself.

His son Richard succeeded him but 'Tumbledown Dick' had no wish to be a dictator and he sensibly resigned and went home to the country. By now even the army realized that the people wanted a king and a parliament as in the old days, and when General Monk marched down from Scotland to arrange matters, there was no opposition to the King's return. On 28th May, 1660, Charles II rode into London amid scenes of joy never known before or since that day.

CHARLES II

THE gallant young man who so narrowly avoided capture after Worcester, had known hard times in exile. Penniless, surrounded by bickering cavaliers and idle companions, he had learnt to hide his own feelings and to trust no one. When he 'came to his own' and recovered his kingdom, he still possessed charm and an easy smile but although he was clever and interested in sport, science and architecture, he was absolutely heartless and seemed to have no aim in life except to enjoy himself. Beneath this lazy good humour there was a hard determination to rule as he pleased and, at all costs, never to be forced to go on his 'travels' again.

The new Cavalier Parliament was filled by the King's friends but although those who had condemned Charles I to death were made to suffer, there was a general pardon for the rest. Indeed, many a brave ruined Cavalier who had lost sons, money and land, complained of the King's ingratitude but, apart from remembering Rupert and some who had helped him to escape, Charles did little for his father's supporters. For the sake of peace and quiet, this may have been wise, but the Cavalier Parliament insisted on passing harsh laws against those who did not conform to the Church of England and who were known as Nonconformists or Dissenters. Some of them, like John Bunyan who began to write *Pilgrim's Progress* in Bedford jail, endured years of imprisonment for their religious beliefs.

The Scots also suffered from these laws. Charles II had no intention of respecting the Covenant, and he not only brought back the bishops to Scotland but allowed them to turn 300 'Covenanter' ministers out of their churches. In south-west Scotland, faithful congregations defied the law by gathering together to listen to their banished minister in some secluded spot on the hillsides. The Earl of Lauderdale, in charge of Scottish affairs, retaliated by sending dragoons to break up the meetings and collect fines at the bayonet's point. Instead of being cowed, the Covenanters broke into open rebellion and some of their leaders were punished by hanging and torture. Hundreds were herded aboard ships and taken into exile in the West Indies.

Early in Charles II's reign, war broke out again with the Dutch. The King's brother, James, Duke of York, Prince Rupert and General Monk were capable admirals and the English seamen fought with their usual bravery, so that for a time, the enemy was held in check. But the navy was scandalously mismanaged. Dishonesty in the shipyards meant that the fleet was badly equipped and forever short of stores and victuals; the sailors' pay was always in arrears and ships which ought to have been at sea were frequently laid up for economy. In 1667, the Dutch succeeded in sailing up the Thames and into the Medway to burn several warships and to carry off the *Royal Charles* as a prize. Furious at this humiliation, the nation laid the blame on Clarendon, the King's unpopular minister, and on Charles's extravagant gifts to his friends and lady-loves, but it was really Parliament's meanness that had brought the navy into such a dismal state.

Before the startling naval reverse at Chatham, the nation had already suffered two disasters in the capital. For many years, a disease known as the Plague was a regular visitor to towns during the summer months, but

in 1665 London suffered an outbreak that was far more
severe than usual. The sickness began unusually early in
the year and, as the weather grew warmer, it increased
at a tremendous rate in the city where filthy streets and
rat-infested buildings were perfect breeding-places for
disease. So many people became ill or panic-stricken
that houses and shops were closed and business came to a
standstill. Deaths rose to close on seven thousand in one
week and, with the churchyards full, bodies had to be
carted away by night to be buried in great pits. The
court and all who could fled to the country, and in the
stricken capital hardly a soul dared venture out of doors:
'Lord, how empty the streets are,' wrote Samuel Pepys

in his diary, for he and stout old Monk had stayed behind, 'and they tell me that in Westminster, there is not a physician left, all being dead.'

With winter's coming, the Plague slowly died away, but in the next year another disaster made the populace feel that the wrath of God had descended upon them. In September, 1666, after a long spell of dry weather, a fire broke out in a baker's shop in Pudding Lane, near London Bridge. Fanned by an easterly wind, the flames leapt from house to house and across the narrow streets until almost the entire city, from the Tower to the Temple, was blazing. Water-buckets, the primitive fire-engines and even the old method of pulling down houses were useless to check such a fire and it was not until gunpowder was used to blow up whole blocks of houses that the flames were brought under control.

In four days more than 13,000 houses, churches and public buildings had been destroyed, besides property valued at nearly ten million pounds. When at last the Great Fire was over, a wonderful opportunity presented itself to build a noble city with wide streets and views of the river. Sir Christopher Wren made such a plan but the owners of houses and shops insisted on rebuilding their property in very much the same places as before. However, brick and stone largely took the place of timber, London became the most handsome capital in Europe and Wren devoted his genius to rebuilding the churches and St Paul's Cathedral.

The rest of the reign was an uneasy tale of plots, discontent and religious bitterness. Charles always admired France and the magnificence of his cousin Louis XIV who, from his sumptuous Palace at Versailles, was intent upon dazzling the world with his military conquests. Alarmed by the French King's ambition, Britain, Holland and Sweden formed an alliance to protect themselves, but Charles made a secret treaty with Louis, promising to help rather than to hinder his plans. In return for a large income, he would use the English fleet against Holland and restore the Roman Catholic religion in England when the time was ripe.

By all the rules of war, little Holland should have been speedily crushed. But at sea the Dutch were a match for the English and on land William, Prince of Orange, fought with stubborn courage, even flooding great areas of his country to check the French armies. When Charles had come to the end of his money, he had to leave France to carry on the war alone but he still kept on good terms with Louis and was able to draw enough money from him to be able to do without Parliament for the latter part of his reign.

But he did not dare to introduce his own religion which he had kept secret for so many years. Riots and plots taught him how deeply, if unfairly, the people hated Roman Catholicism, and it was only on his deathbed that he finally admitted his faith.

JAMES II

BECAUSE Charles II left no heir, his brother James, Duke of York, came to the throne. He started with great advantages, for Parliament voted him a good income for life and he could always count on Louis XIV for friendship. But James was a Roman Catholic and, unlike his brother, he did not keep his beliefs to himself. Almost at once, he made it clear that he meant to favour the Catholics.

A Protestant plan to overthrow James was launched from Holland. The leaders, a Scottish Covenanter called the Earl of Argyll and the handsome young Duke of

Monmouth, decided to raise a two-fold rebellion. Argyll crossed from Holland and endeavoured to raise the Highlands by sending a fiery cross through the glens as a sign to the clansmen to prepare their weapons. Through jealousy and bad management, the rising collapsed and Argyll was taken and executed. Monmouth's rebellion in south-west England was a more serious threat to James.

The Duke landed at Lyme Regis and was proclaimed King at Taunton. Thousands of Protestants came in from the surrounding countryside to join his standard but farm lads armed with scythes and old muskets were no match for the King's soldiers. At Sedgemoor, the royal army repulsed a brave attack by the rebels and then hunted them mercilessly across the countryside. 'King Monmouth' was found hiding in a ditch and although he grovelled piteously before his uncle, he was speedily executed.

The King's vengeance did not end there. He sent Judge Jeffreys down to the west country where, at the Bloody Assizes, this ferocious man gleefully had over 300 persons put to death, including one poor woman whose only crime had been to feed a few exhausted fugitives. Hundreds of others were sent to slavery in the West Indies.

Two risings had been snuffed out so easily that James felt that he could now go ahead with his plans. An army, officered mostly by Catholics, was assembled just outside London, Catholics were appointed to high positions, judges who disagreed with the King were removed from their posts and Parliament itself was dismissed. James then announced what was called the Declaration of Indulgence. This abolished the laws against people who did not belong to the Church of England, and James thought he had made a master-stroke to win over the

Dissenters. But the Dissenters saw through the trap. If they were to be free, so were the Catholics and they feared the Catholics far more than the Church of England. James ordered the Declaration to be read in every church but nearly all the clergymen refused to obey and seven bishops signed a paper telling the King that he was breaking the law. 'This is rebellion,' cried James, and ordered the bishops to the Tower.

As the prisoners were taken through the streets, people knelt down to ask for a blessing and by the time the Archbishop and his six companions were brought to trial, the whole country was seething with indignation. A jury found the bishops 'Not Guilty' and that night the people lit bonfires, rang the bells and placed in their windows seven lighted candles, one taller than the rest. On that same night, some of the leading men of the kingdom sent a message to Holland asking William of Orange to come to England to save their liberties and the Protestant religion.

It was not only the trial of the bishops that brought about James II's overthrow. He had two grown-up daughters, Mary, wife of William of Orange, and Anne. Both were Protestants. But after his first wife died, James had married an Italian princess who was expecting a baby at about the time of the bishops' arrest. The child was a boy and although the story was put round that he was not the Queen's child at all but had been smuggled into the palace in a warming-pan, most people recognized the truth – that James now had a son and heir. This was serious news for the Protestants, because it meant that, unless they acted quickly, England would have a line of Roman Catholic monarchs.

Shortly after receiving the letter of invitation, William of Orange landed at Torbay in Devonshire with a small army and advanced cautiously inland.

James came out from London to oppose the invader but, apart from his Irish troops, he could not rely on his soldiers to fight. While he hesitated, he learned that Lord John Churchill, his best general, had gone over to William's camp and that his daughter Anne had deserted him. At this news, he fled, only to be captured by some fishermen and brought back. His presence was so embarrassing that he was allowed to escape a second time and his sole gesture of defiance was to drop the Great Seal into the Thames as he was rowed down river in a small boat. Without a blow being struck, the Glorious Revolution was over.

Index

THE STORY OF MAUDE REED *by Norah Lofts*   25p

552 52010 1   Carousel Fiction

Her grandfather was only a wool merchant and his house
was not considered suitable for a young girl of noble blood.
Maude was now old enough to be taught the accomplish-
ments of a lady; sewing, music and the art of graceful
behaviour. But this was the Fifteenth Century, and her
school was to be an old dark castle.

HAVELOK THE WARRIOR *by Ian Serraillier*   20p

552 52007 1   Carousel Fiction

These are the days when evil men conspire to overthrow the
monarchy, greedy for the power and wealth of wearing the
crown and ruling the land. The King of Denmark is dead, his
son Havelok forced to flee the murderous attempts of Earl
Godard by escaping to the shores of England. He grows up to
be a great warrior, to recover his kingdom.

EVERYDAY LIFE IN PREHISTORIC TIMES
by Marjorie and C.H.B. Quennell   each 25p

552 54005 6   Carousel Non-Fiction
552 54006 4

This series presents a picture in words of how our forefathers
lived in their prehistoric world, moving out of their caves into
the earliest settlements; discovering metals; making fires;
building and constructing the first organized villages. The
EVERDAY LIFE series follows them, detailing their develop-
ment into civilization as we know it.

DANNY DUNN TIME TRAVELLER
by Jay Williams & Raymond Abrashkin   25p
552 52005 5   **Carousel Fiction**

Inventions and experiments always fascinated Danny Dunn, but somehow anything of a scientific nature had a habit of going wrong as soon as Danny managed to get himself involved. Professor Bullfinch had a new machine, a machine to challenge the boundaries of TIME itself. Danny was determined not to be left out, unfortunately for the Professor.

THE BLACK PEARL *by Scott O'Dell*   20p
552 52008 X   **Carousel Fiction**

The Black Pearl belonged to the old men, with legends and stories to tell to pass the time – or so Ramon Salazar had thought, until he came face to face with the devilfish and the struggle for the pearl began. But Ramon had more than the dangers of the sea to conquer. Others wanted the Great Pearl of Heaven, including the evil Pearler from Seville.

LOOKING AND FINDING *by Geoffrey Grigson*   25p
552 54007 2   **Carousel Non-Fiction**

You can find sunken treasure, hidden away in some long-forgotten shipwreck, or discover the past through scattered fossils and ancient inscriptions. It depends what you're looking for, how you go about finding it. It depends where you're looking, how you go about getting there. But once the search begins, there's no knowing what you might stumble across.

CAROUSEL NON-FICTION PAPERBACK SERIES

All these books are available at your bookshop or newsagent. If you have difficulty obtaining them, they may be purchased by post from **TRANSWORLD PUBLISHERS**. Just tick the titles you want and fill in the form below.

••

TRANSWORLD PUBLISHERS, P.O. Box 11, Falmouth, Cornwall. Please send cheque or postal order – not currency – and allow 5p per book to cover the cost of postage and packing.

NAME ....

ADDRESS..

(SEPT/71) ....